Choosing
a Career in
Carpentry

Carpentry is an important and necessary trade. If you enjoy constructing things with wood, carpentry could be the right career for you.

WAW

Choosing a Career in Carpentry

Allison J. Ross & Scott Harrison

The Rosen Publishing Group, Inc.
New York

In memory of Bob Harrison.

Published in 2001 by The Rosen Publishing Group, Inc.
29 East 21st Street, New York, NY 10010

Library of Congress Cataloging-in-Publication Data

Ross, Allison J., 1974–
Choosing a career in carpentry / Allison J. Ross and Scott Harrison. — 1st ed.
    p.   cm.—(World of work)
Includes bibliographical references (p.) and index.
Summary: Discusses the day-to-day operations, career opportunities, and requirements involved in the field of carpentry.
    ISBN 0-8239-3294-X (library binding)
  1. Carpentry—Vocational guidance—Juvenile literature. [1. Carpentry—Vocational guidance. 2. Carpenters. 3. Vocational guidance.] I. Harrison, Scott, 1973– II. Title. III. World of work (New York, N.Y.)
TH5608.7 .R67 2000
694'.023—dc21   00-009128

Manufactured in the United States of America

AEA-0907

Contents

Introduction

When you think of the word "carpenter," what comes to mind? A toolbelt or hammer? Some wood and nails? Or perhaps you think of a home that is under construction, a chair that needs to be fixed, or some scaffolding on a newly built sky-scraper. Whatever the case, you are probably familiar with some of the things that carpenters do and the kinds of projects that they work on.

The majority of carpenters in the United States work for contractors who build, remodel, or repair buildings and other structures. Carpenters work on a variety of projects, such as public works projects. A carpenter in this area would perform tasks such as constructing wooden forms for pouring con-crete; building wooden bridges, piers, and trestles; and installing tunnel bracing. Other carpenters perform tasks such as building, repairing, or modifying ships, wooden boats, or woodwork inside railcars. But carpentry work can also be found in places you might not expect. Some car-penters, for example, work for manufacturing firms, government agencies, retail and wholesale

The majority of carpenters in the United States work for contractors who build, remodel, or repair structures.

establishments, and schools. Carpenters can even be found in the arts—as set builders in a theater or television production company, or in a museum or art gallery, constructing exhibits.

How can you figure out if carpentry is right for you? As with all career decisions, you must know what is involved in this field before you start a career in it. Tailor your research to what is important to you. If, for example, your main concern is salary, then you should focus on that aspect as you learn about a job. If you are concerned that a job may not be the right fit for your personality, do some research into the characteristics that are necessary to be successful in that job. This should help you make your decision.

Enid's Lesson
Enid thought that her best friend, Sam, had an awful job.

"He owns his own carpentry business, and I couldn't imagine why he would like a job like that," she says. "He spends long hours working by himself, and he often has to work overtime. Plus, if the weather is bad, he can't work, but he still has to find the time to finish the job. I wouldn't want to try to juggle so many projects."

Enid decided to keep her thoughts to herself, thinking that eventually Sam would come to the same conclusions she did. But one day, after Sam had had a particularly rough day at work and was telling Enid all about it, she decided to voice her concerns.

"He seemed so tired and worn out," she says. "I thought that maybe his job had something to do with that, and I wanted him to know that I would support him if he decided to make a career change."

But Sam was shocked to find out that Enid thought he didn't like his job.

"Yes, owning my own business can be hard work," says Sam, "and it often involves long hours and a fair bit of frustration. But what job doesn't?"

Sam realized that he had never expressed to Enid how much he loved his work.

"All she ever heard was the bad stuff," he says. "I never told her what my job meant to me. I love working outdoors, fixing and building things, and helping people out," says Sam. "And the variety of projects I have the opportunity to work on is fantastic. I wouldn't trade this for the world."

As Enid found out, there are many sides to every job. She never realized all the things Sam loved about his work. This is another reason that it is important to do job research. If you can, talk to those who work in the field that you are interested in. That way you will be able to hear all about the latest information—from someone who knows it firsthand.

What It Means to Be a Carpenter

Carpentry has continued to change over the years, largely because of the rise of machine technology. Many advances in the field of carpentry have made the job easier. For example, balloon-frame construction, which makes use of smaller and lighter pieces of wood, has simplified the construction process. Also, concrete and steel have replaced wood for many purposes, particularly in floors and roofs. Whereas carpenters used to use hand tools, they now have the option of using power tools, which are generally easier and faster to use. But as some carpentry tasks in building construction have become easier, other new jobs, such as making forms for poured concrete, have added to the importance of carpenters at construction sites. Thus, carpentry has continued, and it will continue to be an important and necessary trade.

In the introduction, we discussed some of the projects that carpenters work on—everything from building concrete forms to building sets for television production companies. Now let's discuss

A carpenter prepares for a job by reviewing blueprints and discussing a project with a supervisor.

what is involved in the day-to-day operations of a carpenter. As you have already learned, each carpentry task is somewhat different, but most carpentry tasks involve the same basic steps. The first step a carpenter usually engages in is reviewing the task he or she is about to do. This involves reading blueprints and taking instructions from supervisors. If a carpenter is working with others on a particular project, the carpenters will discuss what they are about to do, who will perform what task, and so on. Performing these steps helps a carpenter figure out what type of work will be involved in that particular project. Carpenters must also know some of the local building codes; these dictate where certain materials can be used. Carpenters need to know these requirements so that they can successfully complete their projects.

Next, the carpenter does layout measuring, marking out the location of materials with a carpenter's pencil or marker, and arranges the materials. Once the materials are appropriately laid out and arranged, the carpenter cuts and shapes them as needed.

Can you think of a few types of materials that a carpenter might use? If you thought of wood, plastic, ceiling tile, fiberglass, or drywall, you were correct. As we mentioned earlier, carpenters use hand and power tools, such as chisels, planes, saws, drills, and sanders. After the materials are cut, the carpenter joins them together with nails, screws, staples, or adhesives. In the final step, the carpenter checks the accuracy of his or her work with levels, rules, plumb bobs, and framing squares. These tools help a carpenter figure out the types of adjustments that need to be made. After the carpenter makes the final adjustments, the project is complete.

Very often carpenters work with prefabricated components, such as stairs or wall panels. In these situations, the carpenter's task is somewhat easier. Prefabricated components do not require as much layout work, cutting, or assembly. Also there are generally fewer pieces involved in prefabricated components. These components are designed for easy and fast installation and can generally be installed in a single operation.

Types of Carpentry Work

Carpenters work in almost every type of construction. They cut, fit, and assemble wood and other materials in the construction of buildings, highways, bridges, docks, industrial plants, boats, and many other structures. The jobs they do depend on the type of construction, the type of company, and the particular skills of the carpenter.

As you learned in the beginning of the book, carpenters work on different projects, but many of the tasks they complete follow similar steps. Now let's discuss some of the other options carpenters have, namely, the types of businesses that they can work for—and the different jobs each business handles.

First, it is helpful to know that the construction industry is generally divided into four separate subindustries: residential, commercial, industrial, and public works. These subindustries differ from one another in the types of jobs they offer and in the clientele they serve.

Here are some examples of types of companies you can work for:

Carpenters who work for small homebuilders are usually involved in many different parts of a project.

Small Homebuilder or General Building Contractor

Carpenters who do this type of work are often involved in every part of a project. They may perform tasks such as putting up the framework, walls, and roof of a structure. Also, carpenters who work for a small homebuilder or general building contractor often install doors, windows, flooring, cabinets, paneling, and molding. Working as this type of carpenter also involves tasks like hanging kitchen cabinets and installing paneling and tile ceilings.

Working for a Larger Operation

Doing carpentry work for a larger operation is different from working for a small homebuilder. For one thing, there is more opportunity for specialized work when you work for a larger operation. For example, you might do only one thing, such as roof framing or installing doors and windows. If you do the same type of work, you will become an expert in that particular area.

Working for a Special Trade Contractor

Carpenters working for a special trade contractor specialize in whatever work the special trade contractor does. For example, if a special trade contractor has expertise in the installation of hardwood flooring, this is the type of work you can expect to do. Other specialties include setting forms for concrete construction and erecting scaffolding.

Carpenters Employed Outside the Construction Industry

What sort of work do you suppose you would do if you were a carpenter but worked outside the construction industry? You might do a variety of installation and maintenance work, for one thing. For example, you might perform tasks such as replacing panes of glass, ceiling tiles, and doors. You could also repair desks, cabinets, and other furniture. Depending on the employer, you might also have the option of installing partitions and windows and changing locks.

Rough Carpenters and Finish Carpenters

Generally carpenters do two basic kinds of work: rough carpentry and finish carpentry. Rough carpenters construct and install temporary structures, supports, and wooden structures used in industrial settings. They also construct the parts of buildings that are usually covered up when the rooms are finished. Among the structures built by such carpenters are scaffolds for other workers to stand on, chutes used as channels for wet concrete, forms for concrete foundations, and timber structures that support machinery. In buildings, a rough carpenter would put up the frame and install the rafters, joints, subflooring, wall sheathing, prefabricated wall panels and windows, and many other components.

Finish carpenters, on the other hand, install hardwood flooring, staircases, shelves, cabinets, trim on windows and doors, and other woodwork and hardware that make the building look complete, inside and outside. Finish carpentry requires especially careful, precise work since the final product must have a good appearance in addition to being sturdy. Many carpenters who are employed by building contractors do both rough and finish work on buildings.

Specializing

As mentioned in the introduction, carpenters often specialize in one type of carpentry. Some carpenters build sets for theaters and television studios. Other carpenters build wharves and docks. Millworkers, who work in factories, make prefabricated parts for buildings—such as window frames, cabinets, and partitions. These parts are shipped already assembled to the construction site. Other millworkers are employed by lumberyards, cutting lumber and

Rough carpenters construct and install supports and temporary structures.

building such prefabricated structures as walls, floors, and ceilings.

You might also choose to specialize in cabinet-making if you decide to become a carpenter. Cabinetmakers custom-design cabinets, counters, shelves, and other fixtures for homes, stores, and restaurants. Sometimes, although this is not too common, a cabinetmaker might choose to specialize in building fine furniture by hand.

You may be surprised to learn that some carpenters work with other materials besides wood. These carpenters apply drywall or prefinished covering such as vinyl to ceilings, walls, and partitions. Carpenters can also specialize in applying acoustical panels to soundproof rooms.

Most carpenters are employed by contractors and builders. Those who work in cities often specialize in one kind of carpentry, while carpenters working in rural areas may do many kinds of rough and finish work.

A Carpenter's Working Conditions

*F*rancis went on a two-week vacation with his parents in the summer between ninth and tenth grade. When he got back, he found that most of his friends already had found summer jobs.

"I thought it would be no problem to find a job after I got back from my trip," Francis says now. "But because we live in a small town, and I didn't have any previous work experience, I was having a hard time trying to find a job that I was qualified for. It seemed like all my friends got jobs, and I was left in the dust!"

Soon after the family got back, Francis's mother, Mrs. Kayla, went to lunch with her friend Jan. Mrs. Kayla told Jan about the hard time Francis was having, and as it turned out, Jan thought she might be able to help. She suggested that Francis call her neighbor, Juan, who owned his own carpentry business. Jan had heard he was

Working as a carpenter can be a tough and tiring job, but it can also be rewarding and fun.

looking for an extra hand to help him with some work.

Jan was right—Juan was looking for some summer help. And Francis's call came at just the right time.

"My business was really booming since the weather was good, and I had quite a few projects lined up," says Juan. "I was thinking of hiring someone new, but as it turned out, I didn't have to look too hard since Francis was interested in helping out."

Francis learned a lot in the couple of months that he worked for Juan. He was surprised to find out how tiring it was and how careful he had to be working with the tools and equipment. But he also learned that a job as a carpenter can be extremely rewarding and even fun. He enjoyed meeting new clients and helping people out.

A Tough Job

As you might imagine, being a carpenter can be hard work. As with other jobs in the construction industry, some of the work that you do will not only exhaust you mentally but will take a physical toll as well. For example, you might have to stand for long periods of time while you perform a task. This may not sound too difficult, but try doing it for a few hours and you will see how much it takes out of you!

As a carpenter, you will also have to climb, bend, and kneel to get certain jobs done. These motions can make you tired, and it will take you a while to get used to this aspect of the work. Also, you may be surprised to learn that carpentry can be a hazardous job. As a carpenter, you will often risk injury from slips or falls. Don't forget that you will also have to use sharp and rough materials, which can be dangerous—as can using sharp tools and power equipment.

Rough carpenters work mostly outdoors. As a rough carpenter, you should expect the weather to play a very large role in your job. This means that you might lose work time in the winter and when the weather is cold and rainy. Fortunately, during the winter it is possible that you will be able to take on small indoor jobs. Also, rough carpenters (and finish carpenters, too) can expect to lose time because of layoffs and material shortages.

21

Carpentry can be a physically demanding job. Carpenters often have to bend and kneel to get various tasks done.

Job Conditions

Carpenters usually work as part of a crew, and they sometimes have to work in dusty or noisy conditions. There is no standard length of a job. For example, you might do a house repair that takes you a few hours, or you might work on an industrial construction project that lasts several years. Many carpenters find that they enjoy this variety; it can be just as rewarding to work on a short, simple project as it can be to work on a lengthy one.

Frequently, carpenters find that they have to change their employer each time they finish a construction job. For example, if you are working as a carpenter on a particular project, once that project is complete, you will have to find a different job, and it may involve working for someone else. You can also alternate between working for a contractor and working as a contractor yourself on a small job.

Most carpenters work forty-hour weeks—eight hours a day, Monday through Friday. However, there can be a lot of overtime. Higher wages are paid for overtime work. Generally overtime is available depending on the job and its deadline for completion. As a rule, carpenters provide their own hand tools and work clothing. The employer provides ladders, scaffolding, and any heavy equipment needed on the job.

If you think that you are interested in carpentry as a career, read the next chapter to find out if you have what it takes.

Personal Characteristics

Deciding to go into a particular field is a big decision. You should have an interest in the career—after all, this is something you will spend much of your time doing. But you will also have to make sure you are cut out for the job. Do you think that you have the characteristics that are necessary for this field? Answering the questions below will help you get a better idea as to whether or not you have the right personality for a career in carpentry.

Is a Career in Carpentry for You?

•Are you careful and precise? Are you able to pay good attention to detail?

As you know, building, fixing, and constructing are all activities that require a fair amount of attention. If you are careless, you might not be able to perform your job correctly. Being careful and precise are skills that are important when you are dealing with hand and power tools—being careless could result in an injury.

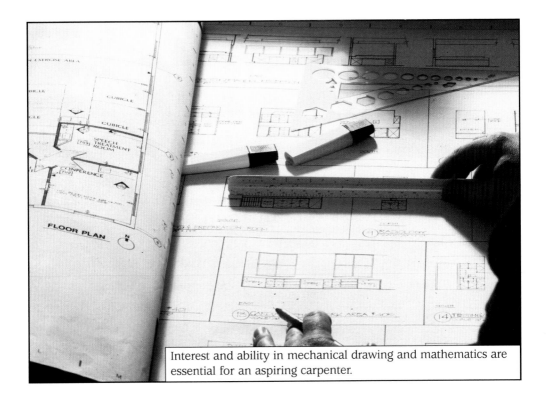

Interest and ability in mechanical drawing and mathematics are essential for an aspiring carpenter.

•Do you have patience and stamina?

As a carpenter, you will likely experience bouts of frustration. As an example, you might not be able to fix something right away, or you might have to think of different options or ways of solving a problem. You will also experience long hours and difficult working conditions, so having patience and good stamina are very important qualities for a carpenter.

•Do you have an interest in courses in woodworking, mechanical drawing, and mathematics?

Are you able to solve arithmetic problems quickly and accurately? As a carpenter, you should enjoy these subjects. You should also like working in these areas. If you hate math and mechanical

25

drawing, for example, this career may not be a good match for you. Being able to solve problems quickly and correctly can help make your job a bit easier.

•Do you have good manual dexterity and good hand-eye coordination?

Because being a carpenter involves working with your hands, these qualities are a must. For example, if you do not have good hand-eye coordination, it may be very difficult for you to assemble something, and because you will be working with hand and power tools, you also face a greater risk of hurting yourself.

•Are you able to imagine how things will look when they are assembled?

Let's say that you are not good at visualizing how things are supposed to look. For one thing, this will make it difficult for you to figure out whether your method of assembly is the best one, or whether what you are planning will actually work. If you aren't able to visualize things well, you may find a job as a carpenter quite difficult.

•Are you strong and in good health?

Being a carpenter requires heavy lifting and the strength to operate tools and equipment, so it is important that you be strong and in good health. As a carpenter, you will also have to do a fair bit of standing, squatting, stooping, bending, and climbing. These positions will be easier to handle if you are in good shape.

Physical strength is required to operate the tools and equipment used in carpentry.

•Are you able to follow instructions well and to take direction from others?

As you have already learned, a big part of being a carpenter is being able to read blueprints and speak with your supervisors about a particular job. If you don't take the time to follow instructions, your project may not work out as you intended.

Noah's Research

Noah, a sophomore in high school, says that he wanted to be a carpenter for as long as he can remember.

"I don't know why exactly, but I never grew out of the stage of wanting to play with hammers and nails," he says, laughing. "My carpentry tool belt was the first toy that I remember playing with for hours on end. I was completely fascinated with it."

That fascination led Noah to the career center one day after school. He had a meeting with his guidance counselor later in the week, and he wanted to make sure that he had done some career-oriented research. He read about a variety of different careers in construction, but carpentry still seemed like the best match for him, and that was what he was most interested in.

"I may not have a lot of practical experience with carpentry, but I possess some of the skills that are necessary for the job," he says. "For example, I am good

Regular physical exercise can help keep you in shape for a career as a carpenter.

at playing video games and I am great at sports—and both of these activities require a mastery of hand-eye coordination. So although I haven't demonstrated this skill using power tools, I know that it is something I am good at. Also, I am in shape; I run and lift weights about three times a week. Math is my best subject, and I enjoy doing it. I love working with my hands and creating things, and can appreciate the amount of detail and attention that even the smallest construction project needs."

Noah's guidance counselor agreed with his assessment. It certainly seemed as though carpentry would be a good fit for someone like him.

Salary and Employment Opportunities

Now that you know the type of work carpenters do, and you have a better sense of the working conditions and the characteristics you should have, it's time to talk about some other aspects of the field. Salary, benefits, and employment outlook are all important pieces of information that can help you decide if this field is right for you.

Salary

Many carpenters join unions. A union is a group that represents the interests of the people who are in the union. For example, if a union feels that a particular type of work is dangerous, they will bring it to the attention of those in charge so that changes can be made. Also, many carpenters are members of the United Brotherhood of Carpenters and Joiners of America (UBC).

The average salary for union workers is about $22,100 a year. Nonunion workers tend to make less than those workers who are part of a union. Highly skilled carpenters can earn over $35,000 a

Many carpenters join a union to protect their interests. Union representation can ensure that members make higher salaries than nonunion workers.

year. As we mentioned earlier, earnings may be reduced on occasion because carpenters lose work time in bad weather and during recessions when jobs are unavailable.

As an apprentice, you will probably begin by earning 50 percent of the qualified craft worker's wage. The apprentice's pay is increased every six months by 5 percent until, in their fourth year, they earn 85 to 90 percent of the experienced worker's salary.

Benefits

Union benefits include paid holidays, vacations determined by the number of days worked, hospitalization, and pension plans. Other benefits are negotiated separately for each union contract. Both union and nonunion benefits include vacation pay, health coverage, and retirement plans. You can also get overtime pay if you work as a carpenter.

Employment Opportunities

Job opportunities for carpenters are expected to be plentiful through the year 2006. However, employment in carpentry is expected to increase more slowly than the average for all occupations during this time. Thousands of job openings will become available each year as carpenters transfer to other occupations or leave the labor force. The total number of job openings for carpenters is usually greater than for other craft occupations because the occupation is large and the turnover rate is high.

Also, there are no strict training requirements for entry, so many people with limited skills take jobs as carpenters. Eventually many of these people leave the field because they dislike the work or because they cannot find steady employment.

Construction activity is expected to increase slowly in response to demand for new housing and commercial and industrial plants. Also, the need to renovate and modernize existing structures means that there will be more available jobs in this field. Opportunities for frame carpenters should be particularly good.

A Changing Field

One factor that may decrease the demand for carpenters is the increased use of prefabricated components, such as prehung doors and windows and prefabricated wall panels and stairs. These prefabricated components can be installed much more quickly. As an example, prefabricated walls, partitions, and stairs can be quickly lifted into place in one operation. As these components become more standard in the field of carpentry, their use will increase; this will likely decrease the need for carpenters as well.

Other changes that are expected in the field of carpentry include the fact that better and more efficient materials are constantly being developed. For example, stronger adhesives reduce the time needed to join materials. Also, lightweight cordless pneumatic and combustion tools such as nailers and drills, as well as sanders with electronic speed controls, will make carpenters more efficient and will help them reduce fatigue. Another benefit to improved tools, equipment, and techniques is that a carpenter will have increased versatility. Carpenters who have a working knowledge of these tools and techniques and are able to apply these skills will have better opportunities than those who can do only the more simple and routine tasks.

Factors to Keep in Mind

Although employment of carpenters is expected to grow over the long run, people entering the occupation should expect to experience periods of unemployment. What do you suppose could be the reason for this? You may be surprised to learn that many factors affect the field of carpentry. For one thing, many construction projects are short-term— meaning that they won't take a long time to complete. So if you work on a project that takes only a month to complete, you will need to line up other jobs when that project is finished. In many cases you will find that it is difficult to line up another job right after one is finished. In other words, there will often be a delay between jobs, so you should expect to be unemployed during that time.

As with many fields and careers, the construction industry is also affected by many outside factors—and we don't just mean the weather! As one example, the construction industry is affected by the state of the economy. More specifically, if the economy is not doing well, a company may be less likely to buy more buildings or to have some renovations done. The state of the economy also affects how people spend their own money. If

Jobs for carpenters are more plentiful in cities that are experiencing rapid economic growth.

unemployment is high and companies are laying off their employees, a person may be less likely to put an addition on his or her house. Thus, during economic downturns, the number of job openings for carpenters declines.

The Role of Geography

Job opportunities for carpenters also vary according to where you are. A city that is experiencing rapid growth will have a greater need for carpenters than a small town with slow growth and a small population. Construction activity matches the movement of people and businesses and reflects differences in local economic conditions. Thus, the number of job and apprenticeship opportunities in a given year may vary widely from area to area. As previously mentioned, the introduction of

In a small town that is not expanding, carpenters may find work scarce. Small projects for friends and family may be the only jobs available.

prefabricated structures has reduced the job opportunities for carpenters, especially for those doing rough carpentry. However, since carpenters build prefabricated structures, many will still be employed in factories.

Milla's Story

In the early 1990s, Milla was doing some on-the-job training for a carpenter in a small town in Illinois. But jobs in her town weren't as plentiful as she would have liked. In fact, most of the jobs she worked on were small projects for her friends and family. Milla got the sense that without her friends' support, she would not be able to find any work at all.

Some of this made sense—sort of. Because of the economic recession in the

1980s—when jobs were scarce, and companies were tightening their belts— new jobs and projects weren't as available. But in many places, the strengthened economy of the 1990s brought hope—and with that hope came new jobs. Companies started expanding again, and people began spending their money more freely. All this translated into good news for the construction industry.

Good news for most places, that is.

"Because I worked in a small town that was not experiencing a rapid level of expansion, it was almost as if the recession was still going on," says Milla.

"My job situation should have improved because the recession was over—but it didn't. I knew that if I wanted to prosper as a carpenter, I was going to have to move."

So Milla did just that. She moved to a town about two hours away, a town that was closer to Chicago and that was rapidly expanding.

"Almost immediately after my arrival, I had a few leads on some new jobs," says Milla. "I had chosen a place that was undergoing a lot of construction and that was doing well economically. Plus, the neighborhoods were so beautiful, and the town was so close to Chicago, that it became an extremely desirable place to live. The construction

opportunities were endless—it seemed like every day a new building was being built, and a new house was being added on to or was being redone."

You should note that Milla's example is an extreme one. It is not always necessary to move to another city or town just to find more work. But it is often easier to find work in places that are doing well financially and that are attractive places to live. Just being in the right place doesn't guarantee you a job, but it is another factor to keep in mind.

6

Job Requirements and Advancement Possibilities

To be a carpenter, a high school diploma is preferred—but not required. While in school, courses in woodworking, mechanical drawing, and mathematics will help you prepare to be a carpenter. If you find that you are not interested in these subjects, this may not be the right career for you.

You may be wondering how carpenters learn their trade. The usual method of learning this trade is through on-the-job training and through formal training programs. Some carpenters pick up skills informally by working under the supervision of experienced workers. Others participate in employer training programs or apprenticeships.

Apprenticeship Programs

Most employers recommend an apprenticeship as the best way to learn carpentry. However, because the number of apprenticeship programs is limited, only a small proportion of carpenters learn their trade through these programs. Apprenticeship

Most employers consider apprenticeship programs the best way for carpenters to learn their trade.

programs are administered by local joint union-management committees of the United Brotherhood of Carpenters and Joiners of America, the Associated General Contractors, Inc., or the National Association of Home Builders.

To qualify for such a program, you should be at least seventeen years old. Apprentices are chosen on the basis of written tests and interviews. It is helpful to know that employers and apprenticeship committees generally look favorably upon training and work experience obtained in the armed services and the job corps. Also, if you are able to get an all-around knowledge of construction through high school courses, you will probably have a better chance of joining an apprenticeship program. Similarly, if you have experience in work related to carpentry—such as in assembling or repairing objects—you will also improve your chances of becoming an apprentice.

So what is the apprenticeship program like? One important thing for you to know is that it isn't a quick program; it takes about four years to complete. More specifically, the program consists of about 8,000 hours of on-the-job training and at least 144 hours of classroom instruction each year. Even though this may seem like a lot of instruction, you will discover that the program will provide you with plenty of on-the-job training. In the classes, apprentices learn structural design, common framing systems, how to read blueprints, and how to lay out buildings. On the job, apprentices learn all the techniques and operations of carpentry from experienced carpenters.

On-the-job training is a less formal experience than classroom instruction, and it really gives you a good sense of what being a carpenter is like. Apprentices learn elementary structural design and become familiar with common carpentry jobs such as layout, form building, rough framing, and outside and inside finishing. They also learn how to correctly use and maintain tools, safety practices, first aid, building code requirements, and the properties of different construction materials. In addition to all that you will learn in an apprenticeship program, you will also learn how to work effectively with members of other skilled building trades. As you may have already guessed, a formal apprenticeship is a terrific way of finding out whether carpentry is really the right field for you.

If you decide not to choose the apprenticeship route, you should know that informal on-the-job training is usually less thorough than an apprenticeship. The degree of training and supervision often depends on the size of the employing firm. For example, a small contractor specializing in home building may provide only training in rough framing. In contrast, a large general contractor may provide training in several carpentry skills. Although specialization is becoming increasingly common, it is important to try to acquire skills in all aspects of carpentry and to have the flexibility to perform any kind of work. Carpenters with a well-rounded background can switch from residential building to commercial construction to remodeling jobs, depending on demand.

Because they are exposed to the entire construction process, experienced carpenters may be qualified to become general construction supervisors.

Career Advancement Possibilities

Now that you know about the type of training that is involved in becoming a carpenter, you might also be curious about the other options available to you with this type of training. As we have already mentioned, it is always a good idea to have a well-rounded background in the field of carpentry. With the right amount of experience and skills, you will have several options. Some of them include:

Carpentry Supervisor or General Construction Supervisor

Carpenters who have experience, skills, knowledge of new developments in carpentry, and good leadership skills may be promoted to

43

Independent contractors have the option of choosing the projects they will work on.

carpentry supervisor or general construction supervisor. Because carpenters are exposed to the entire construction process, they usually have greater opportunity than most other construction workers to become general construction supervisors. As a supervisor, you oversee the operation of the project, manage the crew, and make sure everything is running as it should.

Independent Contractor

As an independent contractor, you can be hired to do your own projects, and you can also be hired to work as part of a team on various jobs. Independent contractors have the option of choosing the projects they will work on and can look for work just for themselves.

Self-Employed Carpenter

If you have enough money, practical experience, and business knowledge, you might become a self-employed contractor; almost one-third of all carpenters own their own businesses. As a self-employed carpenter, you could make cabinets and furniture, do repair work, and remodel houses.

Estimator

An estimator figures costs of materials and labor for a job. To advance to this position, carpenters should be able to estimate the nature and quantity of materials needed to properly complete a job. They should also be able to figure out, with accuracy, how long a job should take to complete and how much it will cost to finish the job.

Certification or Licensing

The United Brotherhood of Carpenters and Joiners of America (UBC), the national union for the industry, offers certification courses in a variety of specialty skills. These courses teach the ins and outs of advanced skills—such as scaffold construction—that help to ensure worker safety, while at the same time giving workers ways to enhance their abilities and to qualify for better jobs. Some job sites require all workers to undergo training in safety techniques and guidelines specified by the Occupational Safety and Health Administration (OSHA). Workers who have not yet passed these courses are considered ineligible for jobs at these sites.

7

Getting Started

*J*an was just twenty-two when she decided that being a carpenter wasn't right for her.

"It was an awful feeling," remembers Jan. "I had just finished my apprenticeship, and I had learned so much while I was completing it. I felt I was really ready to branch out and work in the field, and wanted to work toward owning my own business. I had even won the respect of a lot of people who had thought at first that because I was a woman, I wouldn't be a good carpenter. Problem was, I grew tired of the work. Sure, I loved repairing and building things, but I didn't like the ups and downs of the business. I was interested in having steady work, not in having to find new work when my projects were completed."

Jan didn't know what to do. On the one hand, she had invested so much time learning about the field of carpentry. But *on the other hand, she was worried that she would get stuck working as a carpenter forever if she didn't do something about it soon.*

On the advice of a friend, Jan took some time off and decided to go to the Maritimes in Canada for a week vacation.

"While I was there, I did a lot of sightseeing—and a lot of thinking," says Jan. "I tried to sort out for myself what it was that I was having a problem with. Before I went on my trip, I thought that I was having second thoughts about being a carpenter. And the fact that this was the first time I was having these thoughts—when previously I had been so sure that this was what I really wanted to do—well, that really bothered me."

But Jan realized that it wasn't carpentry that was the problem. Instead, she figured out that she was just going through a transitional phase. She had, after all, just finished her apprenticeship and was about to embark on a new phase in her life: working as a trained and experienced carpenter. As Jan realized, it wasn't carpentry she was afraid of—she was just apprehensive about this new phase of her life.

"And once I had that figured out," says Jan, now a successful carpenter who has owned her own business for

When considering the right career for yourself, it's important to remember that you can always change your mind.

three years, "I felt so much better about everything. I came home from Nova Scotia with a new outlook, I got a job as a carpenter, and now I love what I do."

Changing Your Mind Is Natural

One thing that is important to remember—when you are thinking about the right career—is that nothing is set in stone. For example, let's say that as a teenager, you decide you would like to be a carpenter. But perhaps you will find—and this could happen at any time, even after you have been in the field for years—that this is not the right career for you. Or let's say that you discover that you thought that you would enjoy being a supervisor but that you really prefer being a more hands-on carpenter. While such a realization is likely to be distressing, it isn't the end of the world. Many people change their careers over the course of their lives; it is perfectly normal.

A World of Opportunities

Changes of heart aside, carpentry is a very exciting field to work in. For one thing, you will likely have the opportunity to work outside. This is a nice option for people who would prefer not to spend their day in an office or behind a desk. As we discussed, there are also several options available to you as a carpenter, and this kind of variety can keep things interesting. You could own your own business, work on several different projects, or supervise a crew of workers. One day

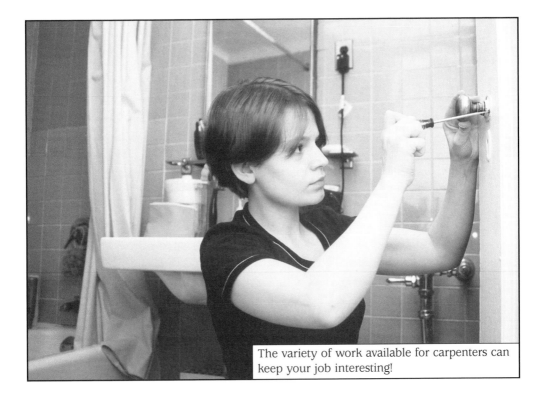

The variety of work available for carpenters can keep your job interesting!

you might find yourself fixing a door or installing a window; another day, you might be adding on a new room to a house. The length of projects also varies, which can keep things interesting—you never know where you will work next!

If you have made the decision to work toward a career in carpentry, you may be wondering how to get started. If you are under seventeen—and thus ineligible to apply for an apprenticeship—you should consider learning as much about the field as you can. But beyond classes like woodworking or mechanical drawing, how can you explore this field? Do not worry, there are many things you can do. First, you can contact trade organizations like the National Association of Homebuilders or the Associated General Contractors of America (see the For More

Information section at the back of this book). Both of these organizations sponsor student chapters around the country, and they can give you some current information.

Another option is to volunteer for an organization like Habitat for Humanity (contact information can be found on page 58). Habitat for Humanity is an internationally recognized nonprofit organization dedicated to building decent, affordable housing in partnership with people in need. Local chapters can be found all over the United States. Their youth programs accept volunteers between the ages of five and twenty-five, and their group building projects provide hands-on experience. A program like this one can help you decide if this career is the right one for you.

There are many other options available to you—you just need to do a bit of research. Do you know someone who works as a carpenter? If you do, you could ask to accompany him or her on a project. This could be a great learning experience for you. Or what about your school? If your school has a drama department, you might consider looking into the possibility of building sets, which can be a fun way to learn simple carpentry skills. You can also try your local home improvement store. Very often this type of store sponsors classes that teach a variety of carpentry skills. You can also take out videos and books from the library, as well as watch television shows that feature programs on the world of carpentry.

In addition to all the things you can do to get experience with carpentry, it is always a good idea

Carpenters can volunteer for organizations like Habitat for Humanity, a nonprofit group dedicated to building decent, affordable housing.

to speak with people who work in the field. Talking to others who have already established themselves—and who have already experienced the pluses and minuses of the job—can help you gain invaluable information about what this job entails. It is also a good idea to speak with those who work in different aspects of the business, such as an independent contractor, a carpenter who owns his or her own business, and an estimator. Ask them what type of work they do, if they are happy with their field, etc. And don't forget to ask them for advice! The people who work in the industry are some of the best resources you will find. The important thing to remember is to get out there. By learning all that you can, you will find the job that is right for you.

Glossary

adhesives Substances that are used to bind one object to another.

blueprints Photographic reproductions, such as those of architectural plans or technical drawings, rendered as white lines on a blue background.

chisel hand Tool with a square, beveled blade used for shaping wood, stone, or metal.

drywall Wall made of prefabricated material. Drywall consists of a thin layer of gypsum that is sandwiched between two pieces of heavy paper (made in standard-size panels of four feet by eight or twelve feet).

fiberglass Textile fabric made from woven glass fibers, used mainly for insulation.

finish carpenters Carpenters who specialize in the finishing details of a structure, such as the trim around doors and windows.

labor union   Group for particular occupations, such as carpentry, that you can join. A union represents the interests of the people in the union. For example, if the union feels that a particular type of work is dangerous, it will bring it to the attention of those in charge so that changes can be made.

layout measuring   Marking out the location of materials with a carpenter's pencil or marker prior to building with them.

level   Instrument giving a line parallel to the plane of the horizon. A level is used for testing whether things are horizontal.

pension   Sum of money paid regularly to a person who has retired.

plane   Tool consisting of a wooden or metal block with a projecting steel blade, used to smooth a wooden surface by paring shavings from it.

plumb bob   Ball of lead or other heavy material attached to the end of a line. It is used for finding the depth of water or determining the angle on an upright surface.

pneumatic tools   Tools that are run using compressed air.

prefabricated components   Preassembled materials that carpenters work with. Prefabricated components are designed for easy and fast installation and can generally be installed in a single operation.

rafter Each of the sloping beams forming the framework of a roof.

rough carpenters Carpenters who specialize in building the rough framing of a structure.

salary Fixed, annual compensation paid to an employee for his or her work or services.

subflooring Foundation for a floor in a building.

turnover rate Rate that represents how often people leave a particular profession to do something else. The turnover rate in carpentry is high, which means that people often leave the industry in order to work in another profession.

For More
Information

In the United States

Associated Builders and Contractors
1300 North 17th Street, Suite 800
Rosslyn, VA 22209
Phone: (703) 812-2000
Web site: http://www.abc.org

Associated General Contractors of America, Inc.
333 John Carlyle Street, Suite 200
Alexandria, VA 22314
Phone: (703) 548-3118
Fax: (703) 548-3119
Web site: http://www.agc.org

Habitat for Humanity International
        Youth Programs
121 Habitat Street
Americus, GA 31709-3498
Phone: (912) 924-6935 ext. 3410
Web: http://www.habitat.org

National Association of Home Builders
1201 15th Street NW
Washington, DC 20005
Web site: http://www.nahb.com

National Association of Women in Construction
327 South Adams Street
Fort Worth, TX 76104-1081
Phone: (817) 877-5551
Fax: (817) 877-0324
Web site: http://www.nawic.org

United Brotherhood of Carpenters and Joiners
of America
101 Constitution Avenue NW
Washington, DC 20001
Phone: (202) 546-6206
Web site: http://www.necarpenters.org/UBC.htm

United States Department of Labor
Bureau of Apprenticeship and Training
200 Constitution Avenue NW, Room North 4649
Washington, DC 20210
Phone: (202) 219-5921
Web site: http://www.doleta.gov/atels_bat/bat.htm

In Canada

Canadian Construction Association
75 Albert Street, Suite 400
Ottawa, ON K1P 5E7
Phone: (613) 236-9455
Fax: (613) 236-9526
Web site: http://www.cca-acc.com

Habitat for Humanity International
P.O. Box 20148
Ottawa, ON K1N 9P4
Phone: (613) 749-9950
Web site: http://www.habitat.org

Independent Contractors and Business Association
    of British Columbia
211-3823 Henning Drive
Burnaby, BC V5C 6P3
Phone: (604) 298-7795; 1-800-663-2865
Fax: (604) 298-2246
E-mail: info@icba.bc.ca
Web site: http://www.icba.bc.ca

Ontario General Contractors Association
6299 Airport Road, Suite 703
Mississauga, ON L4V 1N3
Phone: (905) 671-3969
Fax: (905) 671-8212

Winnipeg Construction Association
290 Burnell Street
Winnipeg, MB R3G 2A7
Phone: (204) 775-8664
Fax: (204) 783-6446
E-mail: info@wpgca.com
Web site: http://www.wpgca.com

For Further Reading

Abram, Norm. *Measure Twice, Cut Once: Lessons from a Master Carpenter.* Boston, MA: Little, Brown, and Company, 1996.

Haun, Larry. *Homebuilding Basics.* Newton, CT: Taunton Press, 1999.

Martin, John H. *A Day in the Life of a Carpenter.* Mahwah, NJ: Troll Communications, 1997.

Sheldon, Roger. *Opportunities in Carpentry Careers.* Lincolnwood, IL: NTC Contemporary Publishing Company, 1999.

Spence, William. *Carpentry & Building Construction.* New York, NY: Sterling Publishing, 1999.

Willis, Wagner H., and Howard S. Smith. *Modern Carpentry.* Tinley Park, IL: Goodheart-Willcox, 2000.

Index

About the Authors

Allison J. Ross was born in Montréal and now lives in New York where she is a writer and ceramist. Scott Harrison is an architect. He spends much of his spare time designing wood furniture.

Photo Credits

Cover © Superstock; pp. 2, 25, 43, 53 © Superstock; p. 7 © John Zoiner/International Stock; p. 11 © Jeff Kaufman/FPG International; p. 14 © Stephen Simpson/FPG International; p. 17 © Keith Wood/ International Stock; p. 20 Tugboat Studios Inc./FPG International; p. 22 © Arthur Tilley/FPG International; p. 27 © Kevin Laubacher/FPG International; p. 29 by Louis Dollagray; p. 31 © VCG/FPG International; p. 35 © Michael Goodman/FPG International; p. 36 © Ron Chapple/FPG International; p. 40 © George Ancona/International Stock; p. 44 © L.O.L. Inc./FPG International; p. 49 © Steve Smith/FPG International; p. 51 by Ira Fox.

Book Design

Geri Giordano

Layout

Danielle Goldblatt